Casualties

Casualties

Poems 1966–68
by J. P. Clark

AFRICANA PUBLISHING
CORPORATION · NEW YORK

Published in the United States of America 1970
by Africana Publishing Corporation
101 Fifth Avenue
New York, N.Y. 10003

Library of Congress catalog card no. 73-113090
SBN 8419-0041-8

Printed in Great Britain

Contents

Part II **Incidental Songs for Several Persons**

For my wife, her mother and Uncle Chris
who gave me sanity and security as did Daddy

We have no gift to set a statesman right.

W. B. YEATS

No metaphor, remember, can express
A real historical unhappiness.

W. H. AUDEN

Casualties

1 Song

I CAN LOOK the sun in the face
But the friends that I have lost
I dare not look at any. Yet I have held
Them all in my arms, shared with them
The same bath and bed, often
Devouring the same dish, drunk as soon
On tea as on wine, at that time
When but to think of an ill, made
By God or man, was to find
The cure prophet and physician
Did not have. Yet to look
At them now I dare not,
Though I can look the sun in the face.

11 Skulls and Cups

'LOOK, JP,
How do you tell a skull
From another?' asked Obi.
'That this, could you find where he fell,
Was Chris, that Sam, and
This there in the sand
Of course Emman. Oh yes,
How does one tell a cup on the floor
From another, when the spirit is emptied?'
And the goblets are legion,
Broken upon the fields after Nsukka.

III Vulture's Choice

THE VULTURE wanted a child
Six years was a long time
To be married and no child
What if the foetus should drop?
Then I shall eat it for breakfast.
What if the wife should die?
Then I shall eat her for lunch.
What if mother and child should die?
Then I shall eat both for the night.
The vulture wanted a child
Six years is a long time
To be married and no child!

iv The Burden in Boxes

BOXES WERE BROUGHT by night
Boxes were left at crossroads
As gifts for the people
Without distinction
With no key to the locks
No bearer at hand to take back
Baskets, take back platters with rabbit ears.

Open the boxes was the clamour
Of monkeys above tides. *Open them all!*
Cows in the plains mooed over grass. But
Into cold storage the high priest
Of crocodiles moved the boxes,
Draping them in sacks muzzled at
The neck, into cold storage
He stowed them of unknown number.

Bring us the bearers of the gifts,
The gifts left us in boxes at
The crossroads, bring them out, we say,
So we may see them in the market place.
But in cold storage he left the lot,
The high priest of crocodiles who skipped
Over hedge in the dark, then leapt back,
Into sharp sunlight, hearing the cheer
Given voice by sea and desert,
Into cold storage he carted the boxes,
All making ominous music on the way.

v The Usurpation

CAUCUSES AT NIGHT, caucuses by day,
With envoys, alien and local,
Coming and going, in and out
Of the strongroom. What briefs
In their cases? The state,
Like a snake severed of its head,
Lies threshing in blood, and
Unless a graft at once is found,
The bird will flee the tree.

VI The Cockerel in the Tale

AT THE DESERT end of a great road
To the sea, he who woke up the lion
And burnt down his den over his crest,
He who the same night bagged
A rogue elephant, not sparing his brood,
He who in heat of that hunt
Shot in the eye a bull with horns
They say never gored a fly, hooves
That never trod on cocoa or groundnut farm,
Stood,
Alone on the trembling loft of the land,
And like the cockerel in the tale, proclaimed
The break of day uncertain then
Where the sun should rise.
He lent the winds of the world
His name, that morning he lent them forever.

VII The Reign of the Crocodile

THEY SAY,
Because the alligator is stark deaf,
He runs as the torrent.
If so, the old master of the stream
Must have had a hundred ears, prickly as leaves
Of the pine before wind-breath,
That summoned by a concourse on the banks
To breast a festival flood,
He punted upon his tail,
And like the whirlpool at Ganagana,
Swallowed his own head.

And so for six months a mighty river
Silted in the mouth,
Lacking distributaries;
For six months fields upon banks
Crackled to the sky,
Lacking distributaries;
And in caves flooded by them
Tied feet and tongue at pleasure of the leopard
And lion, palms peeled at palms.

To acolytes at the same time,
All nearly of one clan, and none
Out of bed when sun at noon
Paced into night, the high priest
Of crocodiles gave places
Right inside the shrine for all tribes,
Yam scrambled in palm oil
That was for gods out of land, sea, and sky.
The people cried for strokes to stem a tide.

With his left he released
To them pigeons and promises.
As if a skyful of pigeons, a sea
Of promises could drown the burden
Heaving now in boxes like pythons.

Of him some scribes have written:
Taking a tour of his castle
By the sea, days
After the usurpation,
From parapet he moved
Into cellar, and
After that, never rose again.

Others wrote:
He came to centre stage,
Straight from the drinkhouse.
Seated long after payment,
The people cried for a song,
The song was in the street,
But like the ham he was,
He sat down to a party,
Called in his cronies, and
Not one knew the song.

WHEN CALABASHES HELD petrol and men
  turned faggots in the streets
Then came the five hunters
When mansions and limousines made
  bonfires in sunset cities
Then came the five hunters
When clans were discovered that were not in the book
  and cattle counted for heads of men
Then came the five hunters
When hoodlums took possession of police barracks
  in defiance of bullets
Then came the five hunters
When ministers legislated from bed and
  made high office the prize for failure
Then came the five hunters
When wads of notes were kept in infant skulls
  with full blessing of prelates
Then came the five hunters
When women grew heavy with ballot papers delivering
  the house entire to adulterers
Then came the five hunters
When a grand vizier in season of arson turned
  upon bandits in a far off place
Then came the five hunters
When men lost their teeth before they cut them
  to eat corn
Then came the five hunters
When a cabinet grew so broad the top gave way
  and trapped everyone therein
Then came the five hunters

At club closure,
Antelopes slept, for lions snored;
Then struck the five hunters,
But not together, not together.
One set out on his own into the night,
Four down their different spoors by the sea;
By light of stars at dawn
Each read in the plan a variant

And so one morning
The people woke up to a great smoke.
There was fire all right,
But who lighted it, where
The lighter of the fire?

Fallen in the grass was the lion,
Fallen in the forest was the jackal,
Missing by the sea was the shepherd-sheep,
His castrate ram in tow,
And all around was the blood of hounds.

ix What the Squirrel Said

THEY KILLED the lion in his den
But left the leopard to his goats
They killed the bull without horns
But left the boar to his cassava
They killed the elephant with his brood
But left the crocodile to litter the field
They killed a sheep who played shepherd
But left the hyrax who was hyena

The rumour sprang seed
In the throat of a squirrel
The seed grew into a trunk
Inside fangs, inside horns
Wind from its blast blew down forests,
And the rage is not done, coils
Of it about us, about our necks.

x Leader of the Hunt

HE WHO BEGAN it all,
Grown mad with love or hiss
Of housewife and harlot,
One night plucked out of bed
A vizier; his treasurer, taken
As well, spilling bags of bills
All the way to a shallow grave
On some wayside. That night, while others failed
Their parts, he left behind a trail
Of brass all loaded with lead,
In the end fled
The prize some swear he plotted for years,
Because of the tryst a confidant
Did not keep. Foiled though through the gates,
He drove across country, blood on
His boots, bodies in his boot,
Unknown to crowds jubilant for a champion.
Kith and kin he had spared, though
More ravenous than lion or rogue elephant,
Denied him then, as they would again and
Again. So back he reeled across country,
Helped over stile by several hands with key
To surgery or bedroom, decked at one point
As a belle, in which guise he crossed
The border, shorn of beard, shorn of sleep,
Never more to wake from nightmare,
Never more know a friend.

There in another country, kept
As a thing of curiosity in a cage

Before a god about to fall,
I held him in my arms,
The friend I dare not look at again,
Though I stare the sun in the face.

xi Conversations at Accra

A: THE SITUATION MAY change,
   It may change completely.
   Then, they who condemning the change
   By force of arms, have inherited
   The booty, may in their turn
   Be divested of the spoil it is plain
   They will feed to birds of the air.
   Brother in fact may turn
   Against brother, and the same act
   Repeated from sea to desert.
   Then may I not return home
   To the people, oh my people,
   Clamouring for a parade
   They know not the leader!

B: The clamour is not in markets only
   The clamour is in cathedrals
   The clamour is from minarets
   And not in the morning alone
   The clamour is in kitchens, in schools;
   In court, in palace alone is silence.

A: Is that so? Is that so?
   Then I am happy, very happy.

C: Dog does not eat dog
   Why in the hunt did the pack
   Fall on its own kind?

A: Because the hounds at the head of the pack
   Played with the lion
   Because they hunted with the lion

Because they hunted for the lion
One gave in fact fangs to the hyrax,
Called into the kennel the jackal.
And another was sent
As plague upon his breed. Oh, rabid
The day the keeper delivered
All in the grassland to the lion,
All in the forest to the leopard,
The breed fell upon every blade
To hand, in defiance of teeth filed
On latest drill, and all along,
All the course swaddled face
In handkerchief, with cheer
The breed carried in its vein rats.

C: Still, crickets and cows are crying
   Whether thongs could not have served
   Where fangs have torn up graves
   None again can cover.

A: You mean tie a thorough hound
   To a tree and set a common cur
   As guard over him? Oh boy, oh boy,
   Before you rush to the next post,
   There would be reversal of rôles, and you
   At the end of the leash.

B: And the penalty is death
   By fang. Oh, broken in town now
   Is the pack, each pouncing on
   The other asleep.

A: It was a pack the trainers left
   Without union of heart or sight.
   Disbandment seems the one course
   It can now run. Look,
   I am a soldier,
   Well able to look after myself
   On the way home by land,
   Sea, or air. But what word
   Have I the general who offers
   Me now in one hand a flag of no colour
   Has not in the other the writ of fire?
   The situation, on the other hand,
   May change, change utterly, and
   New paths open out, whether into day
   Or relapse further into night,
   Which of us here can tell?

C: A group goes hunting as one man
   A hunter goes into the night
   With carbide eye on his head
   His companion his gun
   If one returns home without the other
   Then something is wrong
   The animal lies fallen in the forest
   If shoulders do not bear it home together
   Then something is wrong
   The leader of the hunt is up on the iroko
   Scattered are the group in the forest
   The buffalo stumps over shrubs
   The buffalo stools under the iroko

His tail stirs stool to lash it out
Further up the iroko scales the leader of the hunt
Gathered are the flies on the meat
The people may not eat.

A: I know, I know, don't I know? That night
The group accepted me leader,
Even he who took the lion.
They will follow now if I blow the horn.

B: Then blow, blow it! Right now,
Scattered in the forest are hounds
You led to the hunt.
Stranded in the woods are dogs listening
For the hunter's horn,
And loitering in the square
Are the people hungry for a share.

C: What if the horn is broken?
What if it broke the night
Ropes of sound, ropes of light
Were cut overhead? Can
A horn be put together like cord?

A: That is the point, that is the point.
Out of four unequal pillars
To a barn like bedlam,
One taller than the rest
Together, I sought to build
A new estate of fourteen wings,
Each interlocked with the other
Around an open court.

I sought to post by each gate
A watchdog, summon to service
Hands that never held dirt,
And upon the stool in the hall
I thought to sit a man,
Burnt clean by fires he had
Himself started. Overnight,
Bricks in the act crumble down,
A pack of cards in the hands
Of a delinquent, and straws
In the wind spell no design.

XII Return Home

TOGETHER WITH Chris I brought him home
On clipped wings, on clipped wings,
He who seeing a forest fire,
Turned on a tap the crocodile
Could not stop, unknown to pilot, to crew,
As plain Fred King. There by the green lights
On the ground the red rug was rolled
From under his feet. Engaged elsewhere was
The horse that should have cantered to the midget plane,
Crawling now to its place of rest. Instead, came
A donkey to carry into the night
King Fred, Chris close at his back,
Sam holding to a restive tail,
And I alone on the tarmac
With odd items to clear,
A number of papers I did not dare declare.

xiii The Locust Hunt

LOCUSTS WERE DISCOVERED outside city walls
Locusts were decried in stranger settlements
Locusts were hunted down to women and children
With mortar, matchet, with broomsticks and rackets
In shops, in streets, in offices
Locusts were hunted down in courts and convents.

So a royal bull was slain
With all the egrets on his hump
So dog ate dog in a hunt
With a scattering of the pack in the plain
Oh, how many grasshoppers make up
The loss of one elephant?
How many ticks must there be
To eat up one mastiff?

A river under clear skies
Keeps to its channel, but let
The clouds break, let them break
And ripped below are the banks upon the plains.
And let them remember on the banks
The fire struck by one spark,
In grasslands or forest,
Lights up a stockpile.

xiv July Wake
For Emman and Dorcas Awala

IN THE STREETS the jungle-geared jeeps roar,
Glint of SMG, flare of mortar, tremor
Of grenades occupying ministry
And market, and like hens, men go
To bed with the setting sun, the sun
Setting over the land, afraid
It will set on their individual days.

One night, walls fell upon
A cat in mouse hide, clatter of boots
Over and around his doors,
Barricaded with any block from books
To cooker and radiogram. Four hours
He ran a marathon
In his house, uncheered by faces,
Over hedge, voices over telephone,
And even by the 999 squad
He called in. Harassed as a hen
By hawks when the keeper is
Gone, he clutched at last
For the roof of his caving estate,
With bare fingers to scratch there
A hole, perhaps to the sky. Too late,
The gang in green got him then
By legs lost in loosening pyjama.
Crumpled, they flung him
In his sweat and discharge
Down inside their boot, passed mercifully
By now beyond despatch.

Last night to my right, tonight
To my left side and front, oh,
Let but a car come hooting by,
And I hear in its bonnet the roar
Of leopards amok from the forest.

xv Exodus

THEY FLEE THE altar who in
The ceremony of forging the faggot
Danced round the anvil, swung
The heaviest hammer. Others in the act
Said: 'They ought to have left
Us some bars in the fire,
Some wind in the bellows.' As
If rod bends over or spark goes out
Of its own for others to flourish.
More just perhaps was the charge
The clan carried in its heart
The curse of Aristotle: so fast
Through the furnace, a bubble
Sprang down its middle, that pierced,
Has scattered the cast
So quick through the kiln, so given
To toil, it was
The miracle of a generation.

xvi August Afternoon

IN THE BLIND noon
Shadows shudder,
And a column of rats
Scales over roofs
After cats.

XVII The Rat in a Hole

A COUCHANT LEOPARD in its cage
Is a coil of steel with the catch
In a safe. One day
The creature will break
In face of the keeper.

Cooped in my hole,
I cringe as a rat
Upon a rising mound
Of fear, the forbidden meat
I feed fat on,
My own tail my lash.

In the east is the sun,
Calling all to thunder.

XVIII Dirge

SHOW ME A house where nobody has died
Death is what you cannot undo
Yet a son is killed and a daughter is given
Out of one seed springs the tree
A tree in a mad act is cut down
Must the forest fall with it?
Earth will turn a desert
A place of stone and bones
Tears are founts from the heart
Tears do not water a land
Fear too is a child of the heart
Fear piles up stones, piles up bones
Fear builds a place of ruin
O let us light the funeral pile
But let us not become its faggot
O let us charcoal the mad cutters of teak
But let us not cut down the clan!

xix The Flood

THE RAIN OF events pours down . . .
Like a million other parakeets, cunning
In their havens out on the lee,
I don my coat of running
Colours, the finest silver and
Song can acquire. Not enough,
I unfurl my umbrella, resplendent as any
That covers a chief
At a durbar. It buckles, and will
Fly out of my hand. In the grief
Gusts of rain now over all the land,
I flounder in my nest, a kingfisher,
Whose flockmates would play
At eagles and hawks, but like
Chickens, are swept away
By flood fed from septic tanks, till
Together, we drift and drown,
Who were at home on sea, air, and land.

xx Aburi and After

WITH OLD FACES in my mind
Retired to their wing,
I thought for a long time
They were wringing Jack Gowon's hand,
Wringing his hand for use of a rule
Too broken then in the sand
To flog a fly. Only
When bones were wrenched out of joint
In the court of a stranger,
Did we wake to the scowl
Of implacable masks in the compound,
And a keeper now at attention,
With ankle twisted, and
A prayer in his heart.

xxi The Beast

LONG PRONOUNCED IN tumult underground
But not likely because of antlered heads
To rush out of cracks breaking across
The land, the dragon by five young daemons
Released out of their mad love of the land,
Belches, gorged already with the feast
That creates room as it fills the guts.

Wind from the dragon takes possession
Of masks; dung from the dragon
Makes catacombs of cities and farms;
With mere drippings the dragon set
Rivers on fire, flames of this licks
Mangroves to salt, salt more colic than
Arsenic, and debris damming a whole delta.

In the sunset sky kites of all colours take
The wind, swifts and swallows escort them.
Above, how they scream diving for flags
Of fire rooted to the heart, while below
Breath burns more sulphurate
And blood calcifies into boulders
For brother to hurl against brother.

XXII Death of a Weaverbird

SHOT,
At Akwebe,
A place not even on the map
Made available by Shell–BP,
A weaverbird,
Whose inverted house
Had a straw from every soil.
Clear was his voice as the siren's
Chirp with no fixed hour
Of ditty or discourse . . .
When plucked,
In his throat was a note
With a bullet for another:
I am in contact with the black-kite,
At the head of a flock I have led
To this pass.
How can I return to sing another song?
To help start a counter surge?

XXIII Friends

THE FRIENDS
That we have lost,
May be carried
Deep in our hearts,
But shallow is the burden
When placed beside
The loss to kin.
Though we share with the dead
Club or cult,
Our loss, large as the fellowship
We kept,
Is by that number
Relieved of the load
Which is square upon love.

XXIV A Photograph in *The Observer*

Night falls over them
The young enlisted honey-combed
In the sun
Night falls over them
Statuettes of ebony ganged together
As ibeji at an altar
Night falls over them
Heads of them bald
Bared bodies
Crackling from the tight knot
They throw on the field before
A physician
Night falls over them
And already
They are a cache certified fit
For hurling at the ogre
They all see in the dark
Night falls over us . . .

xxv Benin Sacrifice

AND YET ANOTHER screen is rent
Off our bedside . . .

In the glare before dark,
Two rams are led out,
One already broken and on
A stretcher, the other still strutting
On his own steam . . .

Before a full arena
Adorned by governor, trader, and
Parlour wife, two rams are led
Hooded to stakes, anchored
To barrels of sand . . .

They are strung upright.
One seems at a standstill
With the hour, the other
Rippling as the crowd now
And some sixty years before . . .

Then the priest commanding
Intones the charge, and the latest
Instruments of slaughter stutter out
A message mortal at once to two rams
Now men again in the city of blood . . .

And another screen is rent
Off our bedside.

xxvi Party Song

HERE WE MILL drinking by midnight
Here we mill bobbing by fairylight
Here we mill glowing by dimlight

A floor away
Other drums are beating
Other lamps are burning
In a titanic ball

And through open gates by night and day
Brigades and villages are going out
Like lights over Lagos

XXVII The Casualties
To Chinua Achebe

THE CASUALTIES ARE not only those who are dead;
They are well out of it.
The casualties are not only those who are wounded,
Though they await burial by instalment.
The casualties are not only those who have lost
Persons or property, hard as it is
To grope for a touch that some
May not know is not there.
The casualties are not only those led away by night;
The cell is a cruel place, sometimes a haven,
Nowhere as absolute as the grave.
The casualties are not only those who started
A fire and now cannot put it out. Thousands
Are burning that had no say in the matter.
The casualties are not only those who escaping
The shattered shell become prisoners in
A fortress of falling walls.

The casualties are many, and a good number well
Outside the scenes of ravage and wreck;
They are the emissaries of rift,
So smug in smoke-rooms they haunt abroad,
They do not see the funeral piles
At home eating up the forests.
They are the wandering minstrels who, beating on
The drums of the human heart, draw the world
Into a dance with rites it does not know

The drums overwhelm the guns . . .

Caught in the clash of counter claims and charges
When not in the niche others have left,
We fall,
All casualties of the war,
Because we cannot hear each other speak,
Because eyes have ceased to see the face from the crowd,
Because whether we know or
Do not know the extent of wrong on all sides,
We are characters now other than before
The war began, the stay-at-home unsettled
By taxes and rumours, the looters for office
And wares, fearful everyday the owners may return,
We are all casualties,
All sagging as are
The cases celebrated for kwashiorkor,
The unforeseen camp-follower of not just our war.

XXVIII Night Song

THE NIGHT FOR me is filled with faces,
Familiar faces no season
Of masks can cover. Often,
The strange and young I never met,
Like Nyananyo, Amangala,
Boro, all summoned from office
Or study, from sound of highlife
And sweet taste of tongues, straight into
The siren arms of war,
Intercept the faces I loved,
And sun is blotted out that I
Believe should ripen the land anew,
Though the sowing is of hearts I knew
And hold closest still in my head.
Now winds gallop through the gates
Of their eyes. In pots their mouths make
In fields already forgotten
In the fight, grow arum lilies,
Hedges of ivory about them. Let
Me but close my eyes, and they flower
Into more mornings of faces
I dare not look at,
Though I have sat it out in the sun.

The faces recur,
Out of the iron siege of the earth,
Bright bulbs tied to tree hands
Flailing in a storm none
On either side can tell the end. One,
Trapped in a cell when the crocodile

In turn was trussed seated into a hole,
On his return to day, fell
Into a pit. Others, touched on
A chord resonant to the root,
Followed, at the great crossroads,
A dance into the forest. Oh,
How can woods echo a song
That filled city-halls?
How can cantors of the song
Abandon the service on the floor?

A song was begun one night;
The song should have begun
A festival of three hundred tribes.
Instead it lit for cantor
And chorus a funeral pile.
In the crash of columns and
Collapse of rafters,
Another,
Ignored by all as dumb,
Catches the strain, in
The daze of noon the song rises,
Burns down the old ramparts
Of the heart, and before
Smoke seal our eyes, mud our mouths,
Firm upon the ground appears the house
Of our dream, with a mansion
For them who followed ghosts
Into the forests of night.

Incidental Songs
for Several Persons

Incident at the Police Station, Warri
(After *The Flagellation of Jesus* by Piero della Francesca)
For Father O'Flannagan

STRIPPED TO HIS penis, the convict at
His lordship's command is shooed out
Of his cell into the square to a bench,
Gleaming with grime in the sun.
'Lie down!' cracks the order, and at that,
Superfluous uniform hands as of an octopus
Grapple the prisoner down, one smart
Sergeant mounting his back. Now with the hiss
And beat of a cobra incensed,
The big stick descends deliberate and
Constant upon the shivering buttocks till
Carbolic water, blood, and tears, wrung
Free in spite of iron will,
Flow in one polluted stream, washing
Society of another individual wrong.
And the smell
Fills the air of the first flagellation with thong:
The scared, curious throng,
Mainly of women and children, twittering
At the sight of a tail shrunken
Between thighs, three very important
Looking persons discussing in one corner,
Perhaps the latest list of promotions or
Prices on the market, and in a car
Parked close by, one gallant and another
Asking the girls to more wine and song.

The Lagos–Ibadan Road before Shagamu
For Sam, Sesan, Kayode and the Wives

A BUS GROANED uphill. Trapped
In their seats, fifty odd passengers rocked
To its pulse, each dreaming
Of a different destination.
GOD'S TIME IS THE BEST, read
One legend. NO CONDITION IS
PERMANENT, said another. And on,
On over the hill Shittu
Drove the lot, a cloud of Indian hemp
Unfolding among his robes. With
The swish over his shoulders, it
Trailed out, touched tails with the smoke
That squatted all indigo
On the hillside: like a stream
Was the going downhill, swift
Past recollection, straight into a bend
Upturned as a saucer, and
The journey spilt over in a ditch.
In the early morning sun,
To the clamour of flies that first
Answered the alarm, water
Of sewage kind washed their common
Wound, silenced their common groan.

> *No need of first aid,*
> *All died on the spot,*
> Said the dailies. *The police,*
> *Well supplied with notes,*
> *Are looking for the driver*
> *Who escaped unhurt.*

A Lamp by my Window
For Ayo Ogunsheye and Nekan Ademola

I HAVE A lamp
  By my window at night
Dislodges the moon.
  Broken there as a mosaic,
It strikes me in bed
  Each is as many discs
Dancing in a stream
  Bearing me to sleep.

To my Academic Friends
who sit tight on their
Doctoral Theses and have
no Chair for Poet or Inventor

YOU WHO WILL drive forward
But look to the rear mirror
Look at the crashes and
Casualties holding up traffic
To the market. He drives
Well who arrives
Again and again with fresh goods.

Letter from Kampala
To Ebun

AT THIS OTHER end of Africa
It is of you alone
I think at home,
And the children:
I go farther in order
To get home to you.

Nairobi National Park
For Nyambura and James Ngugi

OSTRICH AND GIRAFFE peek
Over bush; warthog and
Baboon amble across roads;
From lone tree to Songora
Ridge drift the heifers,
But shy in the grass
The lion lies,
And placid are the ponds
In Embakasi Plain.

Addis Ababa
For Mary Dyson

BUFFALOES,
Assorted and gelded,
Scramble up burning mountains:
In the lead,
A dinosaur out
Of the Abyssinian lake.

A God is the Cow
For Primila and Charles Lewis

A GOD IS the cow
In India, never to be eaten
As is holy flesh by
Another clan.
Which is not to say
Her children deny
Her. Upon her neck is the common
Yoke for beggar-cart and plough.

The Players

UNION OF BLOOD or need, boy and girl
Carry in their bag no trick
As the old couple in the act.
Natural mishap is the ware
The young hustle in the street.
Thrilled today at the dazzle
Of a rupee the girl can only touch
On the way to a shallow till,
The beggar boy moves scene
For hag to play drum
Majorette to her man, caught
In a cycle-wheel and sundry kit.
How often has staff hurtled
About that crooked bole,
Flogging out of routine a trembling
Flush? Gathered are her palms
Unfolded into a bowl
After drill, but bored are
The itinerant crowds caged in
Themselves. And the flickering
In her eyes is not of the wind.

Bombay

HERE NOTHING SEEMS new: the rising
Estate is cancelled out by septic slums;
The very docks that gave this city
Her name Gateway to India
Smell of the old company
That made paupers of moguls;
The streets crawl with vintage
Vehicles: bullock carts, horse carts, iron
Carts, human carts, all in unison groan
For service. From gardens hanging on
A hill to a mosque afloat
In the harbour, mansion and
Shack tumble down like monsoon
Waves in the Bay of Bengal,
And all about,
Upon monument as upon men,
Grime with slime sits brandishing rags
In wake of an empress now slut.

Calcutta

COW AND MAN loll about
In lice, share in streets
Of slime the same bed
And bath, as the palaces
And slums in flood.

Preface to Notes

The following explanatory notes on the poems have to do with events and persons, some dead, some living. They also pertain to places, beliefs, and customs. It is well to add that all the factual information about the first of the traumatic changes of government my country has experienced came into my hands after the act. Reacting to all the events as I have done in these poems, I want it therefore understood that I had no previous or prior knowledge of the facts or plans, nor am I altogether convinced I have all of them correct and complete. But I got so close to a number of the actors after the curtain rose, actors some of whom still evoke such mixed response, that I came to be identified by some as playing in the show—to the extent of being interrogated by the security people. The pity is that I have had no part at any time in the drama still unfolding. The most I have done is rush the stage at one point, moved by a simple impulse to help a friend in a bad state of nerves after taking on the lead in a play he could not finish. He had not shown some of us his script for fear of independent criticism and rejection. Partly because the paths of poetry are not open to many, and partly because it was the fashion at one time in Nigeria to play the guessing game of who knew what and who did what, even when to speculate could mean danger of possible detention and death, I sometimes wish I had written in prose this personal account of some of the unspeakable events that all but tore apart Nigeria, as pieced together from fragments given by friends directly affected and as they have hit me in passing.

Notes

Skulls and Cups

line 1   *JP*   The poet himself.

line 3   *Obi*   Dr. Obiajunwa Wali; graduated from University of Ibadan and Northwestern University, Evanston; was teaching at the University at Nsukka when the Nigerian Civil War broke out and the town fell on July 12, 1967 to Federal forces under Col. Muhammed Shuwa; fled with others to Enugu, then home to Port-Harcourt where he was during the fall of the town in May 1968 to Federal forces under Col. Benjamin Adekunle; now Commissioner for Rehabilitation in the Rivers State.

line 5   *Chris*   The poet and publisher Christopher Okigbo; born in 1932 in Ojoto near Onitsha in what is now the Central East State; graduated at University of Ibadan, killed in action as a major at Akwebe in September 1967 in the Nsukka sector of the Nigerian war, fighting on the secessionist side.

line 5   *Sam*   Sam Agbam; entered the Diplomatic Service of Nigeria after graduating at Ibadan in 1960; executed in Enugu September 1967 for pro-Federal activities.

line 7   *Emman*   Major Emmanuel Ifeajuna: leader of the Army revolt of January 15 1966 that toppled the civilian government of Sir Abubakar Tafawa Balewa; was held in detention along with other executors of the *coup* by Major-General Aguiyi-Ironsi who himself was overthrown on July 29, 1966; released by the then military Governor of the former Eastern Region of Nigeria Lt. Col. Chukwumeka Odumegwu Ojukwu; executed in September 1967 for planning a counter-*coup* to return Eastern Nigeria to the Federation.

line 11   *Nsukka*   The university and town of that name.

Vulture's Choice

Vulture's Choice   The parable of choice facing the five majors of the *coup* and the country they wanted to save, as told by Major Dom Okafor to Major Emmanuel Ifeajuna.

The Burden in Boxes

The Boxes In the first flush of the *coup*, Nigerians saw it as a gift from the gods, but when the coffins began to be counted, the Pandora character of the gift became apparent. Killed were the civilian leaders Sir Abubakar Tafawa Balewa, the Prime Minister of Nigeria, his party leader Sir Ahmadu Bello, the Sardauna of Sokoto and Premier of Northern Nigeria, their allies the Premier of Western Nigeria Chief S. L. Akintola, and Chief F. S. Okotie-Eboh of the Mid-West Region, the Federal Minister of Finance; and killed also were the senior Army officers Brigadier Zak Maimalari, Brigadier Ademulegun, Col. Shodeinde, Col. Pam, Lt. Col. Lagema and Col. Unegbe—a pattern of killing partial to the Eastern axis of the country. It changed the complexion of the *coup*, although a man of character other than General Ironsi's could still have rescued the situation for the country.

The Usurpation

line 4 *Strong-room* One of the first things Major-General Aguiyi-Ironsi did upon inheriting the *coup* (which he called a mutiny) was to move into the Nigeria Police Control Room at Obalende, Lagos.

The Cockerel in the Tale

The Cockerel Major Chukwuma Kaduna Nzeogwu, in the eyes of the world, the leader of the *coup* of January 1966.

The Reign of the Crocodile

The Crocodile or 'the old master of the stream' (line 4). Major-General Aguiyi-Ironsi was famous for his swagger-stick, a stuffed crocodile.

line 10 *Ganagana* an Ijaw island with a UAC trading station on the River Forcados, one of the main distributaries of the Niger.

Seasons of Omens

Seasons of Omens Nigeria, right from its year of independence in 1960, tottered under terrible misrule but continued to be praised by her 'traditional friends' in the West as 'a showcase for democracy in Africa'.

What the Squirrel Said

The squirrel safe in the bush, is oracle to the python below; counter also to the python into whose folds it drops nuts.

The Leader of the Hunt

Leader of the Hunt Major Emmanuel Ifeajuna. After failing in Lagos, he fled to Accra from where Christopher Okigbo and I brought him back to Nigeria on February 16, 1966, a week before the Ghana *coup* that overthrew President Kwame Nkrumah. Chris was the official emmisary, my rôle a personal one.

Major-General Aguiyi-Ironsi, who wanted all the executors of the *coup* rounded up—whether for court-martial or collaboration, he could not make up his mind—already had Major Nzeogwu brought down to Lagos from Kaduna, after an open accord between the two.

In the uncertain wake of the January 15 *coup* when everyone who had relatives or friends in the Nigerian Army was anxious about their personal safety, I found that Major Ifeajuna was one of the executors of the *coup* and that he had escaped to Accra. As from that point, a number of us, his friends, though angry that he had not consulted us and taken us into confidence before taking his supreme action, felt strongly that he should be found out since—

  i. His escape to Ghana carried connotations of a complicity with or possible directives from Kwame Nkrumah, thereby giving ideological colouration to a *coup* which the country accepted as an act of God
  ii. As an officer, if he was involved, then, we thought, he ought to stand up to the consequence of his action and be by his comrades, especially
  iii. As comments were already beginning to go round that he was only acting in character, running away after disrupting authority, as he had done while a student at Ibadan and Onitsha during the incidents of burglar-grille breaking and strike in both institutions.

Conversations at Accra

The characters here are Major Ifeajuna, Christopher Okigbo and I. Major Ifeajuna is certainly character A, stating the case he would have put up at a court-martial, but characters B and C are larger than Chris and me, being representative of the numerous voices then debating the merits and demerits of the *coup*. Festering in the mind of the Major was the part played by the police and the army in putting down, on behalf of politicians in power, popular uprisings first by the Tiv and then by the Yoruba peoples in what are now the Benue/Plateau and Western States of Nigeria. It is part of the tragic irony of the Nigerian drama that the dreams of the January Majors are the very ones General Gowon took over for Nigeria, namely, the insistence upon the preservation of the unity of the country, the creation of more equable states out of its four ill-balanced regions, the release and invitation to office of Chief Obafemi Awolowo, the use of civilian commissioners respected by the people, and the purging of public life.

Return Home
line 6   *Fred King*   Major Ifeajuna travelled home under an assumed name.
line 11   *a Donkey*   Instead of a senior military officer and member of the Supreme Military Council promised, a junior police officer from the Special Branch met the Major and took him into detention.
line 16   *A number of papers*   Major Ifeajuna left with me on the night of our arrival at Ikeja the manuscript of his account of the *coup*, which after due editing was rejected by the publishers as early as May 1966 because it was a nut without the kernel.

The Locust Hunt
In May 1966 there was the first outbreak of civilian violence and killings in the then Northern Nigeria in protest against the unification decree and generally abortive régime of Major-General Aguiyi-Ironsi.

July Wake
The days were full of terror, confusion and general uncertainty following the openly retaliatory *coup* on July 29, 1966 in which Major-General Johnson Aguiyi-Ironsi was overthrown and killed together with the gallant Military Governor of Western Nigeria, Lt. Col. Adekunle Fajuyi, as well as several officers and men. This was when Christopher Okigbo and I last met—on one of those critical days in August. Partition was the theme then in the air. Chris and I agreed that we must go home, as it was a time

when anybody could be killed by mere association and for the acts of others; but home to him meant Enugu in the East while for me it was Warri in the Mid-West.

Once home, I discovered that partition of the country would not stop at the boundaries of region nor of tribe, but would go to the last unit of clan and of village as obtained in large areas of the country before the British came. And so too would be the division of assets and liabilities. For example, the oil that flowed under much of the dispute and sparked it off into the open flames of secession and war, by the very logic of derivation, should revert not just to one region which, like the rest of the country, was an artificial creation and conglomeration of different and disparate peoples, but to the villages and clans out of whose soil the foreign companies are tapping it for their own gain. And even before the regions came, the country had been. Therefore, after a brief period of shock and doubt, I returned in September to Lagos firm in my belief in a federal Nigeria in need of re-structuring and reform.

Exodus
The movement home of Nigerians of Eastern origin began after the May killings in the North; arrested briefly by appeals from authorities on all sides, it became a mass retreat for military personnel as well as civilians of that region following the second military *coup* of July 29.

Dirge
From late September into early October 1966, in the midst of talks in Lagos to determine the future of a country about to disintegrate, more massacres broke out in the North as reprisals against reported killings in the East.

Aburi and After
Early in the New Year, after the East had pursued for months a policy of 'pulling apart', Nigeria's military rulers eventually met—outside their country—at Aburi, on the outskirts of Accra, under the auspices of Lt. General Ankrah, then Chairman of Ghana's National Liberation Council.

line 4 *Jack Gowon* Major-General Yakubu Gowon whose real claim to history, to my mind, is his picking up and piecing together again the broken pieces, which at once made the Nigerian army and nation.

The Beast
On July 6, 1967 war broke out at last, although secession had been proclaimed on May 30.

Death of a Weaverbird
Christopher Okigbo, of his volume of poems *Limits*.

A Photograph in *The Observer*
line 6   *Ibeji*   wooden twin figures revered by the Yoruba.

Benin Sacrifice
On June 27, 1968, two field commissioned officers of the Nigerian Army in the Asaba and Onitsha sector of the war were found guilty of murdering four Nigerian civilians and executed.

line 17   *Some sixty years*,   The exact figure is 71. In 1897 after the famous British Punitive Expedition to Benin, a number of the city's nobles were executed in the same square for their part in the so-called massacre.

The Casualties
Chinua Achebe   In the thick of the July 29 takeover in 1966, Chinua and I offered each other on the telephone a place of refuge, without actually meeting. We met in London late August 1968 at the offices of a mutual friend and publisher—strangers apart, on opposite sides of the Nigerian rift.

Night Song
line 5   *Boardman Nyananyo*   was born in September 1932 in Brass; studied at Fourah Bay College Freetown and graduated in Maths at St. Andrews, Scotland; gave up teaching at Warri to join the Nigerian Army as a lieutenant after the fall of the Mid-West to the secessionists; killed in action in the Bonny sector on December 7, 1967.

George Amangala   was born 1936 at Oloibiri in what is now the Rivers State of Nigeria; a historian, graduated in Dublin; gave up teaching at Warri at the same time and for the same cause as his compatriot Nyananyo to join the Nigerian Army; killed in action as a captain in the Bonny sector on January 31, 1968.

line 6   *Isaac Adaka Boro*   was born in 1936 at Odi, Rivers State; first came into the news as the student leader at Nsukka who took Sir Abubakar Tafawa Balewa, then Prime Minister of Nigeria, to court for allegedly misconducting the country's census; declared the first secession in Nigeria —of the Rivers State from the then Eastern Nigeria in February 1966 with himself as head of state; rebellion crushed by Major-General Aguiyi-Ironsi; later tried and condemned to death; reprieved by Major-General Yakubu Gowon on August 3, 1967; enlisted in the Nigerian Army as a lieutenant in September 1967 along with compatriots like Amangala, Nyananyo, Sese, and old colleagues like Nottingham Dick; killed in action as a major near Okrika as Port Harcourt was falling a few miles away in May 1968.

line 47 *Another ignored by all* . . . Major-General Yakubu Gowon. While I was an undergraduate at Ibadan, I had known him as a lieutenant through an old friend, Brigadier David Ejoor, the first Military Governor of the Mid-West. I asked Major Ifeajuna in Accra what had happened to Lt. Col. Gowon whom I had not seen for years. His reply was that he had not thought enough of my friend to include him in his plans. Surely a case of the rejected stone becoming the head of the corner!

Nairobi National Park

In July 1968, with a grant from the Farfield Foundation in New York, I went to Australia to attend the Conference of Commonwealth Literature held in August at the University of Queensland, Brisbane, taking the opportunity to do a round-the-world trip that took me in six weeks through Uganda, Kenya, Ethiopia, Pakistan, India, Burma, Thailand, Malaysia, Singapore, Australia, the Philippines, Hong Kong, Japan, the United States of America, Great Britain and Germany. Apparently, I responded most to India—the India of the Bombay steel merchant, S. L. Jajobia, my old friend Emeritus and National Professor Suniti Kumar Chatterji and Neil O'Brien, both of Calcutta, who were all very kind to me.

SOURCES OF INSCRIPTIONS

'On Being Asked For a War Poem', The Wild Swans at Coole (*Macmillan*, 1919).

'The Truest Poetry Is the Most Feigning', Shield of Achilles (*Faber*, 1955).